The T♥ddler's First 150 animal handb♥♥k

BY ASHLEY LEE

e ENGAGE BOOKS
VANCOUVER

e ENGAGE BOOKS

Mailing address
PO BOX 4608
Main Station Terminal
349 West Georgia Street
Vancouver, BC
Canada, V6B 4A1

www.engagebooks.com

Written by: Ashley Lee
Edited by: A.R. Roumanis
Illustrations by: Julian Rodriguez
Proofread by: Katherine Velliquette

FIRST EDITION / FIRST PRINTING

LIBRARY AND ARCHIVES CANADA CATALOGUING IN PUBLICATION

Lee, Ashley, 1995–, author
    The toddler's first 150 animal handbook
written by Ashley Lee ; edited by A.R. Roumanis.

Issued in print and electronic formats.
ISBN 978-1-77437-389-7 (hardcover)
ISBN 978-1-77437-390-3 (paperback)
ISBN 978-1-77437-391-0 (pdf)
ISBN 978-1-77437-392-7 (epub)
ISBN 978-1-77437-393-4 (kindle)

1. Animals—Juvenile literature
2. Vocabulary—Juvenile literature
3. American Sign Language—Vocabulary—Juvenile literature
I. Roumanis, A. R., editor
II. Title.

LCC QL49 .L442 2020 DDC J590—DC23
C2020-027594-1 C2020-027595-X

4 BODY PARTS

6 PETS

9 FARM

14 UNDERGROUND

16 FOREST

20 ARCTIC

22 OCEAN

28 GRASSLANDS

36 BUGS

40 EQUATOR

42 BIRDS

46 ACTIVITY **3**

Nose

Paw

Tail

Feather

Ears

4

Fin

Claw

Whiskers

Antlers

Beak

Wing

Mane

5

Pets

Cat

6 Ferret

Rabbit

Fish

Guinea Pig

Hedgehog

Goldfish 7

Dog

Rat

8 Gerbil

Budgie

Farm

Pig

Horse

Pony 9

Donkey

Sheep

10 Emu

Cow

Chicken

Rooster

Turkey

Goose 11

Goat

Llama

12 Duck

Guinea Fowl

Alpaca

Ostrich

Peacock

Mule 13

Underground

Groundhog

14 Bat

Ant

Mole

Fennec Fox

Worm

Badger 15

Forest

Cougar

16 Possum

Wolf

Bear

Deer

Fox

Snail 17

Toad

Eagle

18 Skunk

Porcupine

Racoon

Chipmunk

Squirrel

Beaver**19**

Arctic

Snowy Owl

20 Sled Dog

Walrus

Orca

Reindeer

Polar Bear

Penguin **21**

Ocean

Hammerhead Shark

22 Salmon

Otter

X2

Crab

Hermit Crab

Shrimp

 X2

Lobster

Clownfish

Blue Whale

24 Shark

Sea Lion

Sea Turtle

Seahorse

Dolphin

Starfish 25

Octopus

Clam

26 **Eel**

Jellyfish

Stingray

Squid

Swordfish

Catfish 27

Grasslands

Elephant

28 Buffalo

Armadillo

Tarantula

Rhinoceros

Hippopotamus

Boar **29**

Gazelle

Scorpion

30 Koala

Panda

Wallaby

Hyena

Sloth

Lion 31

Crocodile

Gecko

32 Tortoise

Lizard

Giraffe

Zebra

Cheetah

Mouse 33

Kangaroo

Camel

34 Vulture

Wild Dog

Tasmanian Devil

Flamingo

Platypus

Tapir 35

Bugs

Grasshopper

36 Ladybug

Termite

Butterfly

Caterpillar

Dragonfly

Firefly 37

Centipede

Mosquito

38 Wasp

Praying Manti

Fly

Bumble Bee

Spider

Moth 39

Equator

Iguana

40 Snake

Tiger

Tree Frog

Chameleon

Parrot

Jaguar 41

Monkey

Orangutan

42 **Gorilla**

Chimpanzee

Birds

X2

Woodpecker

Bluejay

Pigeon 43

Stork

Swan

44 Pelican

Quail

Robin

Crow

Hummingbird

Pheasant 45

activity /

Match the following to the pictures below.

Can you find:
a cat,
a monkey,
a starfish,
a squirrel,
a duck,
a bumble bee,
an elephant,
a penguin,
and a worm?

penguin /

bumble bee /

squirrel /

elephant /

worm /

duck /

46

monkey /

cat /

starfish /

Explore other books at www.engagebooks.com

ENGAGING READERS — LEVEL T — FIRST WORDS
Available in other languages!

FARMER · TREE · APPLE · STAR
HOUSE · DOG
HAND · BALL
SHOES · TRUCK
MOON · BABY · RED · JUMP

The Toddler's
First 150 sight words handbook

ENGAGING READERS — LEVEL T — FIRST WORDS
Available in other languages!

HELICOPTER · EXCAVATOR · FIRE TRUCK · SCHOOL BUS
TRACTOR · AMBULANCE
DUMP TRUCK · BIPLANE
BULLDOZER · PIRATE SHIP
MUSCLE CAR · TUG BOAT · POLICE CAR · TRAIN

The Toddler's
Trains planes + automobiles and things that go
handbook

ENGAGING READERS — LEVEL T — FIRST WORDS
Available in other languages!

EAGLE · CHIMPANZEE · STARFISH · DOLPHIN
ZEBRA · PANDA
DOG · TURTLE
PENGUIN · CLOWNFISH
TREE FROG · LION · BUTTERFLY · ELEPHANT

The Toddler's
First 150 animal handbook

ENGAGING READERS — LEVEL T — FIRST WORDS
Now available in 20 languages!

NUMBERS · COLORS · SHAPES · ABCs
OPPOSITES · SIZES
FOOD · ENGINES
SOUNDS · TIME
ACTIONS · SPORTS · BODY · EMOTIONS

The Toddler's handbook
With over **100 Words** that every kid should know

ENGAGING READERS — LEVEL P — EARLY CONCEPTS
Includes 15 basic concepts!

ABCs · NUMBERS · COLORS · SHAPES
MUSIC · SCHOOL
MANNERS · MATCHING
BIKING · GARDENING
JOBS · ARTS · BRUSH TEETH · POTTY

The Preschooler's handbook
With over **300 Words** that every kid should know

ENGAGING READERS — LEVEL K — READY FOR SCHOOL
Includes 14 basic concepts!

ABCs · COLORS · MATH · SHAPES
VOWELS · TIME
SEASONS · SENSES
WEATHER · RHYMES
CALENDAR · PATTERNS · SCHOOL · CHORES

The Kindergartener's handbook
With over **300 Words** that every kid should know

LARGE 8.5"X11" SIZE! — LEVEL T — AGES 3-4
With activities throughout!

The Toddler's
WORKBOOK
ABC
1 2 3 4 5 6 7 8 9 10
Z
Alphabet, Numbers, Shapes, Sizes, Patterns, Matching, Activities, and More!

LARGE 8.5"X11" SIZE! — LEVEL P — AGES 4-5
With activities throughout!

The Preschooler's
WORKBOOK
A A A A
a a a a
1 5 10 15 20
Alphabet, Numbers, Shapes, Sizes, Patterns, Matching, Activities, and More!

LARGE 8.5"X11" SIZE! — LEVEL K — AGES 5-6
With activities throughout!

The Kindergartner's
WORKBOOK
A Z
a a
1 5 10 15 20
Alphabet, Numbers, Shapes, Sizes, Patterns, Matching, Activities, and More!

Have comments or suggestions?
Contact us at: alexis@engagebooks.ca

Show us how you enjoy your #engagingreaders. Tweet a picture to @engagebooks for a chance to win free prizes.

www.ingramcontent.com/pod-product-compliance
Lightning Source LLC
Chambersburg PA
CBHW051233020426
42331CB00016B/3358